The FOODIE'S
COLOURING BOOK

Jess Lomas and Alicia Freile
Illustrated by Haylea Bridle

Published by:
Wilkinson Publishing Pty Ltd
ACN 006 042 173
Level 4, 2 Collins St Melbourne, Victoria, Australia 3000
Ph: +61 3 9654 5446
www.wilkinsonpublishing.com.au

International distribution by Pineapple Media Limited
(www.pineapple-media.com)   ISSN 2205-1082

National Library of Australia Cataloguing-in-Publication entry

Creator:	Freile, Alicia, author.
Title:	The foodie's colouring book / Alicia Freile and Jess Lomas.
ISBN:	9781925265514 (paperback)
Subjects:	Food--Pictorial works.
	Coloring books.
	Cooking.
Other Creators/Contributors:	Lomas, Jess, author.
Dewey Number:	641.5
Layout Design:	Alicia Freile, Tango Media Pty Ltd
Cover Design:	Alicia Freile, Tango Media Pty Ltd

Custom illustrations by agreement with Haylea Bridle.
Recipe photography by agreement with Jess Lomas.
Cover image of hand with pencil by agreement with iStock.

Jess Lomas is an author and editor from Melbourne, Australia. Her previous titles include *Low Sugar – Collected Edition*, *Diabetes Recipes* and *Real Food Treats*. Jess is a "foodie in training" according to the How much of a foodie are you? quiz in this book, you can follow her on Instagram @jesslomas where she promises she posts more than what's on her plate.

Alicia Freile is a graphic designer and author originally from the United States, and transplanted to Australia. She has written *E-Reader Digest*, a consumer guide to e-readers and e-books. Alicia is the Design Director of Tango Media Australia and USA. Her website is www.tangomedia.com.au.

Haylea Bridle is a freelance illustrator and designer based in the Blue Mountains, Australia. She has a somewhat inconvenient desire to be surrounded by children's books, dairy foods and caffeine in all incarnations, at all times. As an illustrator, she has an open relationship with all mediums, but particularly fancies ink and watercolours, and is often found playing third wheel to their sumptuous marriage.

▶ Coconut butter is a delightfully creamy and naturally sweet spread that's easy to make at home with the help of a food processor. It's important when buying shredded or desiccated coconut for this recipe to check the package for no added sweeteners and ideally no anti-caking agents. It is possible to find packaged coconut with 100% coconut listed on the ingredients list, to keep this snack as pure as possible.

Coconut honey butter on apples

— SERVES 6 —

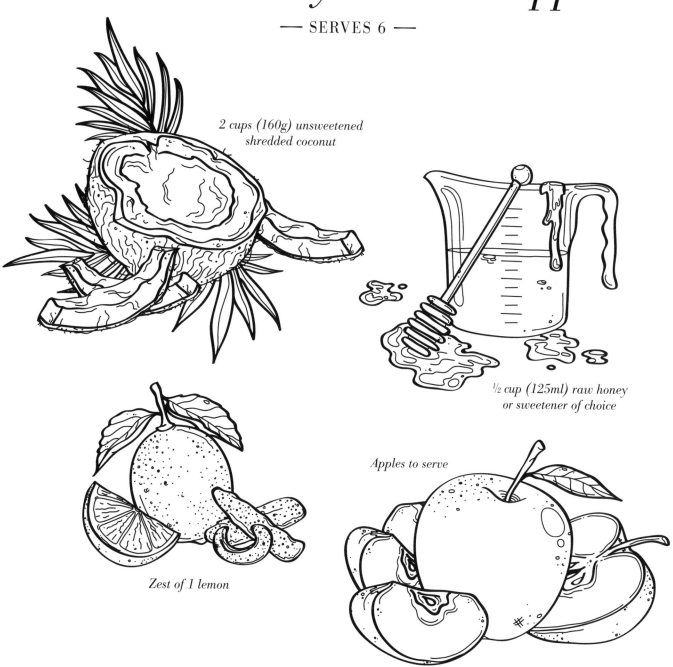

2 cups (160g) unsweetened
shredded coconut

½ cup (125ml) raw honey
or sweetener of choice

Zest of 1 lemon

Apples to serve

1. Place the shredded coconut in the bowl of a food processor fitted with the S blade attachment, or in a blender. Blend on high until the coconut begins to form a paste, you may need to stop occasionally to scrape down the sides of the bowl.

2. Add the honey and lemon zest and continue blending until a smooth consistency forms. If the mixture looks too dry keep going as it can take a while for the butter to form depending on your food processor or blender. You may add ¼ cup (60ml) of water or coconut milk to thin the consistency of the butter out if you like.

3. Slice the apple into quarters or smaller and drizzle a small amount of fresh lemon juice over the top to stop the flesh from browning. Add 1 tbsp of coconut butter to each apple wedge and serve.

Introduction

Welcome to the wonderful world where food and colouring unite! Adult colouring books have taken the world by storm as we look for new ways to relax and de-stress from the pressures of work, family and finances. There are colouring books filled with mandalas, cats, cities and underwater scapes, amongst a plethora of others. Why shouldn't there be a foodie's colouring book that celebrates all that's great about food and food trends?

Foodie has become a word that causes many people to cringe. "You enjoy food? We get it!" they yell. But often the people who say that *don't* get what food really means to those who love it most. Food can be much more than the meals you slap together on a weeknight or the takeaway you have delivered when the fridge is empty. It's more than the single ingredients you place in your shopping basket, and it's more than the newest restaurant that takes months to get into too. Food can be a celebration, a gathering with loved ones or a meal shared over a table of new acquaintances. A food trend can cross the globe; food can be medicine, food can be fuel, food can be fun, absurd, overpriced, a bargain, a cultural experience, a learning experience – the possibilities are exciting and expansive.

In *The Foodie's Colouring Book* you'll find colouring pages that celebrate diverse foods from cakes and sweets to oysters. The A-Z foodie alphabet presents food items, trends or something silly and fun. Opposite each illustration is a short explanation of what is featured, to help expand your knowledge about everything from agar-agar to the end of the kale trend. As a special bonus we've included a bunch of sweet recipes to tempt your tastebuds and give you something to snack on while you colour away your day.

Some colouring books will guide you about colours or materials to use on the illustrations but we'd prefer to let you take the reigns on that. Your cupcakes can be multi-coloured, shaded, cross-hatched, inside the lines or outside them, whatever takes your fancy. This book is a celebration of all that is delicious and fun about food, we hope you enjoy this culinary colouring experience!

▶ This wholefood, vegetarian substitute for gelatine was discovered in Japan in the late 1650s-early 1660s. It's produced from a red algae and is flavourless, odourless and colourless, and can be used to thicken jellies, jams, preserves, sauces and soups. Agar-agar is also the sea vegetable that keeps on giving; it can be used as a laxative or digestive aid, is used in diet products as it gives the sensation of fullness, and is even used at times to make dental impressions.

Not a Star Wars character but a naturally occurring substitute for gelatine made from algae

How much of a foodie are you?

So just how big of a foodie are you? Do you splurge on the hottest restaurants and know the latest food trends or are you a home cook that loves food but doesn't know a cronut from a cruffin? Take the foodie quiz, tally up your points and turn to page 128 to read your results.

1. What does food mean to you?

a. Food is fuel, it doesn't need to be enjoyable. (1 point)

b. Food is life and every meal should be an adventure. (3 points)

c. Food is great but the company you dine with is just as important. (2 points)

2. You open your kitchen cupboards, what do you see?

a. Stale crackers, salt, and what looks like the beginning of a science experiment. (1 point)

b. A mini supermarket of nuts, seeds, flours, spices and sauces. You want it – I have it all. (3 points)

c. It depends on what day of the week it is but I always have enough to make a pasta dish. (2 points)

3. Which scenario best describes you?

a. I am the go-to in my friendship group for restaurant recommendations. (3 points)

b. I look up reviews of a restaurant online before dining there. (2 points)

c. I don't really care where I eat. (1 point)

4. It's payday, how do you celebrate?

a. Make a booking at the hottest new restaurant in town. (2 points)

b. Order a pizza to be delivered. (1 point)

c. Head to your favourite specialty grocer and stock up on flavoured salts, biodynamic yoghurt and gourmet deli meats. (3 points)

5. How many cookbooks do you own?

a. Do newspaper lift outs count? (1 point)

b. I'm not exaggerating when I say 100, I read them like novels. (3 points)

c. About a dozen. (2 points)

6. Who is your favourite celebrity chef?

a. Ronald McDonald. (1 point)

b. Heston Blumenthal. (3 points)

c. Julia Child. (2 points)

7. How should ice cream be made?

a. I don't know I just buy it at the supermarket. (1 point)

b. Using liquid nitrogen, of course. (2 points)

c. By an artisanal ice cream maker who takes risks with flavours, like carrot and habanero pepper. (3 points)

8. How do you enjoy your curry?

a. From the local takeaway shop. (1 point)

b. Cooked at home from scratch. (3 points)

c. Cooked at home but from a jar. (2 points)

9. What's your ideal Frankenstein food experiment?

a. Cronuts. (2 points)

b. Ramen burgers. (3 points)

c. Breakfast for dinner. (1 point)

10. What is Instagram for?

a. Posting photos of every meal you eat. (3 points)

b. Posting photos of your life, which may include food from time to time. (2 points)

c. Posting photos of your baby or dog. (1 point)

▶ Bone broth is a great addition to your daily diet for a number of reasons. Firstly, it's extremely economical to make. Secondly, bone broth is packed full of minerals that we often miss out on in our diets that are more centred on fillets of meat and not the whole animal. Studies suggest that including bone broth in your diet helps you better absorb other proteins, and the gelatine extracted from the bones is great for your joints, skin and hair. Make a batch of bone broth by simmering grass fed beef bones with ¼ cup (60ml) of apple cider vinegar, onion, carrot and celery in enough water to cover the contents of the pot for 8-16 hours on low. Freeze the broth in ice cube trays and heat a few cubes up for a warming and nourishing treat.

Beef water

▶ Julia Child needs no introduction to a true foodie. She was the American chef responsible for bringing French cuisine to the American people with her bestselling book *Mastering the Art of French Cooking*. Child was also described as America's first celebrity chef due to her various television shows, including *The French Chef*, which ran from 1963-1973. More recently she was portrayed by Meryl Streep in the feature film *Julie & Julia*. As Julia would say, bon appétit!

"If you're afraid of butter, use cream."

– JULIA CHILD

▶ Once an exclusive experience for tourists visitng Asian, African or Latin American countries, adventurous restaurants are now offering diners a close encounter of the crawly kind. Ants, crickets, grasshoppers and cockroaches are lean and high in protein, offering a crunchy treat for those willing to try something new. Around 80% of the world's population enjoys eating insects regularly and now the Western world is joining in on the fun. Try a grasshopper taco today!

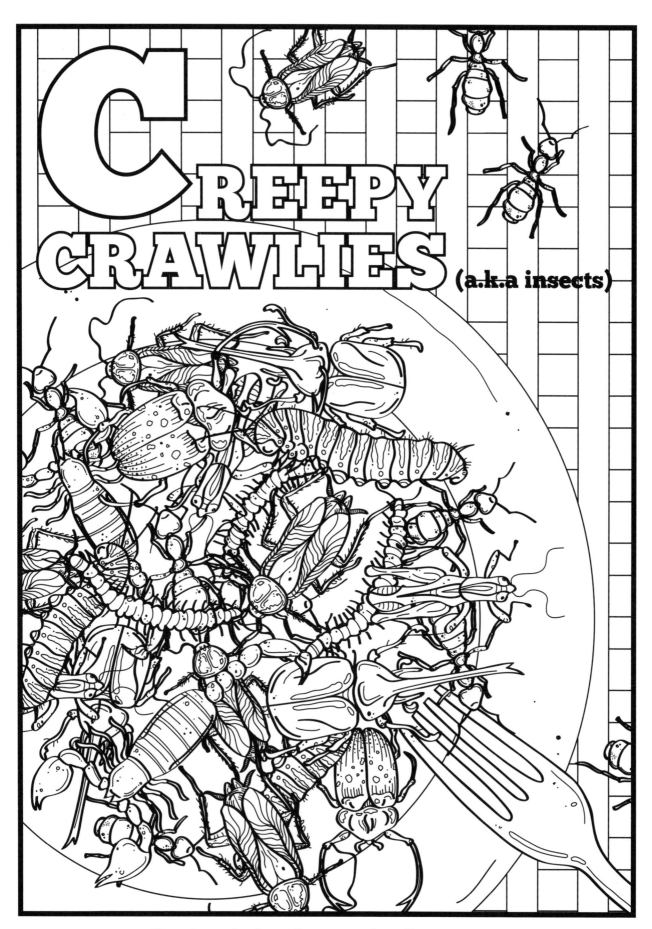

CREEPY CRAWLIES (a.k.a insects)

Eat them before they scuttle off your plate!

▶ Delicious breakfast ideas don't come easier than this.
Taking inspiration from the Mediterranean, where longevity
and happiness are directly attributed to lifestyle and diet, this
breakfast plate can be enjoyed any time of the day. Use what
you have on hand to customise, or add any combination of the
following: continental or Lebanese cucumber, kalamata olives,
mixed green leaves (such as spinach and lettuce), feta cheese,
fried or scrambled egg, hummus, sesame seeds, lemon juice
and extra virgin olive oil.

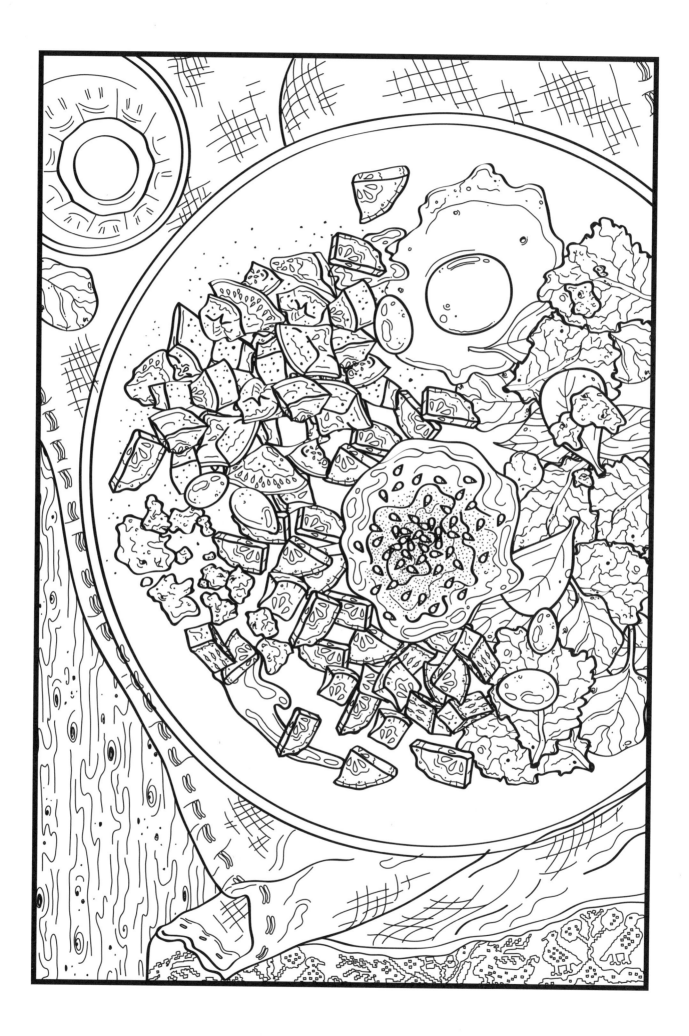

▶ Vegetarians and vegans rejoice! Researchers at Oregon State University's Hatfield Marine Science Center have cultivated a domesticated strain of dulse (a type of algae) that is said to taste exactly like bacon. Not only is this great news for people who don't eat pork for ethical or religious reasons, but it's also great environmental news as dulse is a quick-growing plant that is more ecologically friendly than rearing livestock. Dulse is a superfood that boasts double the nutritional benefits of kale and is high in protein and antioxidants. While it's unlikely you'll be able to buy a bunch of it in your supermarket any time soon, chefs have already begun experimenting with the ingredient, including adding candied dulse chips to ice cream

Bacon of the sea

▶ There are few sights in this world as glorious as a fully stocked cake display. Yes, you can keep your "breathtaking" sunsets and landscapes, a foodie is more interested in the cupcakes, brownies, pies and slices on offer in their favourite bakery or cake shop. From a country cookie to a French macaron, these sweet treats are nothing short of inspirational.

▶ Everything 80s is new again! This food trend was last
seen in the 1980s, amongst the shrimp cocktails, quiche,
wine coolers and pasta salad, but is set for a modern
revival thanks to the rising trends of Nordic food and
foraging. Adding edible flowers to your dish can make
your plate look pretty but they should only be used if also
adding something to the overall taste or eating experience.
Pair lavender and lamb, borage and fish, or oven dried
sugar coated rose petals and vanilla ice cream. Try wild
garlic flowers, chive flowers, zucchini/courgette/squash
blossoms, elderflowers, hibiscus, camomile, nasturtium or
marigolds amongst many others.

Edible flowers

A rose by any other name would taste as sweet

▶ This brunch salad pairs the best of breakfast with the best of lunch. It combines an oozing poached egg on top, roasted tomatoes, revitalising greens, nutty fresh avocado, tender roast chicken, and a zesty lemon dill sauce. Poaching eggs can be a daunting task and many an egg has been sacrificed to the poaching gods in kitchens around the world. If going freestyle isn't your idea of a fun time in the kitchen, use a poaching pod or bag. To make the lemon dill sauce, whisk together 2 tbsp extra virgin olive oil with 2 tbsp fresh lemon juice, 1 tbsp fresh chopped dill, a pinch of sea salt and a good grinding of black pepper.

▶ You can thank (or blame) America for the food truck epidemic sweeping the world. The origins of the food truck date back to the 1800s, more recently they gained popularity in the 1950s on US Army bases, and today they can be seen on street corners globally. The rise in popularity of street food, coupled with economic downturn, saw the food truck trend explode. Now you can find a food truck to cater for any taste, from burgers and tacos, to Brazilian, Greek, pasta, pizza, ice cream and doughnuts.

Why dine at a restaurant when you can eat a taco in the gutter?

▶ You may think sushi as a food trend in the Western world is terribly passé but it's what ingenious chefs are doing with sushi today that keeps this Japanese cuisine relevant and popular. One LA restaurant, Culichi Town, is taking fusion food to a whole new level with their Mexican sushi. While they still use seaweed and rice, their fillings take a more Mexican flavour with steak, chicken, shrimp, cream cheese and avocados.

▶ "Freedom is not worth having if it does not include the freedom to make mistakes." Mahatma Gandhi said this, and the original quote of course made no mention of bagels. Gluten free is still very much on trend in the food world for those with serious gluten intolerance and those who believe they have serious gluten intolerance. More often than not, seeing "gluten free" on packaging or a menu guarantees a customer can be charged double what the gluten-filled item on offer costs.

Freedom is not worth having if it does not include
the freedom to eat bagels

▶ Ernestine Ulmer was an American author born November 7, 1892. There is little to no information available online about her and her Wikipedia page merely informs us she was born into a family of Russian immigrants and died in 1987 in South Dakota. She liked Korean pop music ... we may have made that up. Ernestine's quote is plastered on bakery walls around the world and can be an excellent reminder to look for and enjoy the best life has to offer, we're here for a good time not a long time.

"*Life is uncertain.*
Eat dessert first."

– ERNESTINE ULMER

▶ Dear Sriracha, I hope this letter finds you well. By now you must have heard the news, there's a new hot sauce in town. Please don't take this personally, we still really love you, we just want to mix things up a bit. We can still remember the first time we tried you. We were warned to just use a little bit but we told everyone we could handle our heat. Then our lips burned and we fell in love with the Rooster sauce. Don't cry because it's over, smile because it happened.

Sriracha is out, harissa is in!

▶ A simple tuna salad can be a big crowd pleaser if you take the time to cook a tuna steak. Most homemade tuna salads opt for a can of tuna but for a fraction more effort you can wow your guests (or just yourself) with seared tuna fillets. Pair the tuna with diced cucumber, red onion, fresh herbs and lightly pan-fried cherry tomatoes.

▶ It's hard to remember a world where we didn't all take photos of our food before eating but such a world did exist, and not that long ago. When Instagram was launched in October 2010 it changed the foodie world forever. Suddenly you could share where you were dining or what you were cooking, eating, or lusting over in the culinary world. Most importantly it was judgment free. Perhaps we've taken it a bit far now, with many people expressing frustration over having to wait for a photo to be taken before they can tuck into their meal. Some restaurants have also frowned on the practice while other chefs are overjoyed their cooking is getting more exposure and validation than it has before.

INSTAGRAM

If you don't take a photo of it, does it really exist?

▶ Time to get creative! The aim of the game is just to let loose, draw what you feel and don't be too self conscious - there's no judgment here! You can draw leafy greens, tomatoes and corn, or make up your own plants - perhaps you've always wanted your own gummy bear tree and milkshake shrub?

Finish the Drawing: Sketch in the plants to these roots

▶ Jeroboam is not just a great name for a band, it's also one of the larger style bottles of wine that is sure to kick-start your party! There are two sizes of Jeroboam; while the sparkling wine holds 4 standard bottles, the still wine Jeroboam holds an impressive 6 regular wine bottles - this works out to be 4.5 litres of fun!

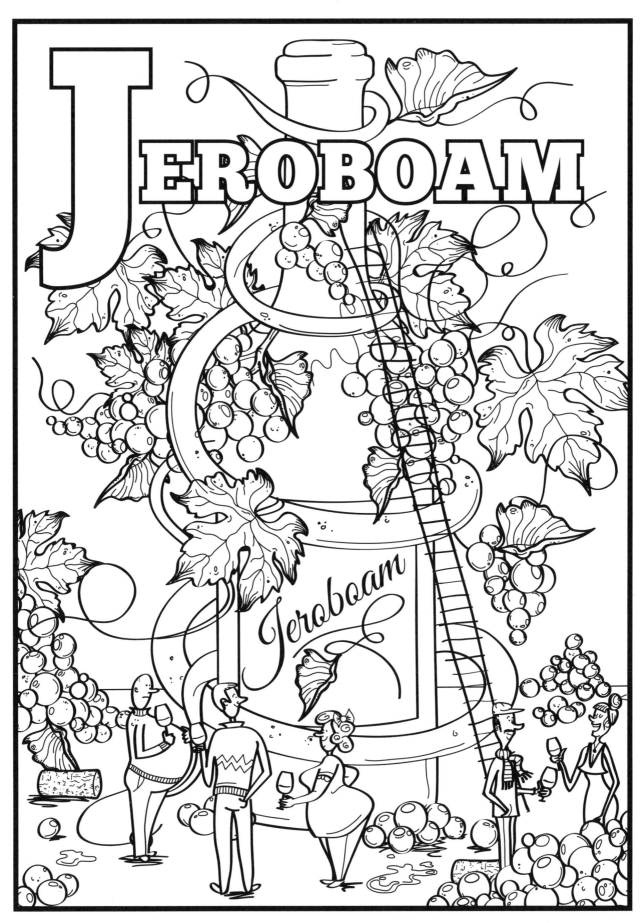

Fee-fi-fo-fum, I smell a drink that's six times the fun!

▶ This is a refreshing, hydrating snack or light meal during the warmer months. You can omit the feta cheese and keep the skewers dairy free, or try substituting other melon or fruits in place of the watermelon.

Watermelon, cucumber + feta skewers

— MAKES 6 —

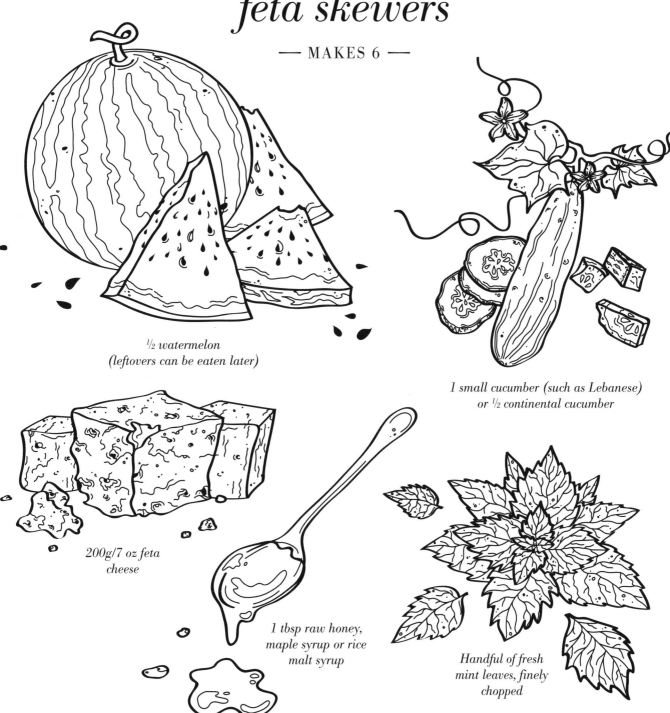

*½ watermelon
(leftovers can be eaten later)*

*1 small cucumber (such as Lebanese)
or ½ continental cucumber*

*200g/7 oz feta
cheese*

*1 tbsp raw honey,
maple syrup or rice
malt syrup*

*Handful of fresh
mint leaves, finely
chopped*

1. Remove the watermelon flesh from the rind and dice into even sized cubes.

2. Leave the cucumber skin on and cut into even sized chunks.

3. Dice the feta into cubes then place in a bowl and add the sweetener of choice and the fresh mint, toss to coat.

4. Thread alternating cubes of watermelon, cucumber and feta onto the skewers until all used up. Store in the fridge.

▶ Once the darling of the superfood world, kale has had a rough time of late convincing people that she's still cool. If anyone's to blame for kale's fall from stardom it's us, the fans. We hyped her and overused her, putting her in salads and smoothies and baking her into chips. Kale is still one of the healthiest vegetables you can eat however so while you may not want to publicly flaunt it as much as you have previously, still try and include some in your diet on a weekly basis.

Adjective used to describe something as passé or overused.
"Those culottes are so kale Jenny!"

▶ The history of the sultana and the raisin is a particularly engrossing one for fans of dried fruit the world over. There were two young brothers, Sultana and Raisin, who were enjoying a bunch of grapes out in the summer sun one day when they were called inside for dinner. They left the remaining grapes where they had been sitting and went inside, only to forget about the grapes entirely. When they went looking for them a few days later they found several small, brown objects where the grapes had been. On a dare Sultana ate one and discovered they were delicious. They began drying bunches of grapes and selling them to the community but they couldn't agree on a brand name. This indecision took a bitter turn when an American company offered to buy the boys out for their idea. Sultana wanted to remain grass roots and local but Raisin was lured by the dollar signs and signed the idea away for exclusive US rights. The brothers never spoke again. Today, depending on where you are in the world, you may enjoy a raisin or a sultana without knowing the drama and heartache that went into such a small piece of food.

▶ The lobster roll is an expensive food trend that's hard to resist - buttery chunks of fresh lobster nestled in a warm hot dog style bun has us drooling just thinking about it. The lobster roll dates back to as early as 1929 in Connecticut, USA but can be found around the world today. The food trend peaked in 2014 in the United Kingdom and Australia but something this delicious never really goes out of style with discerning foodies.

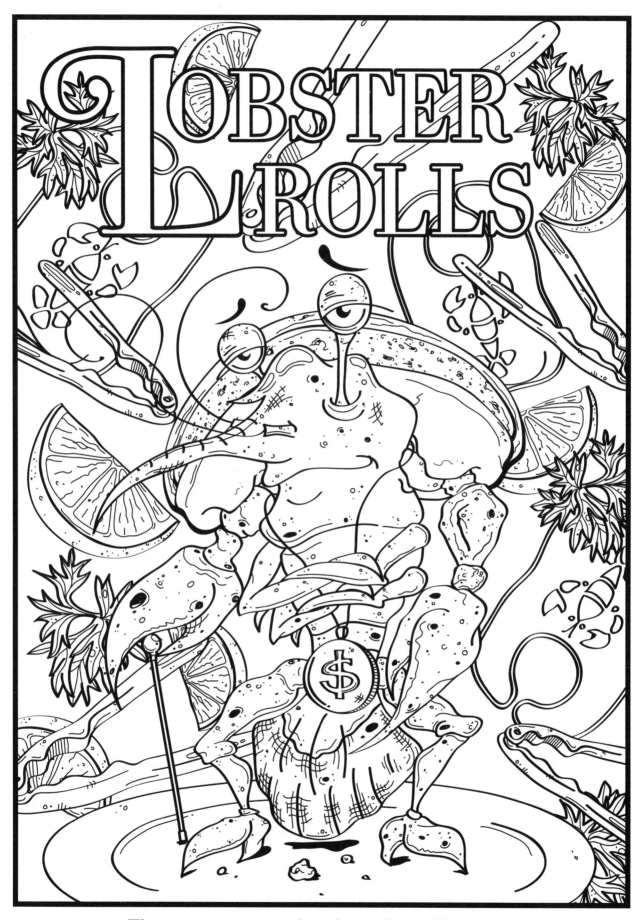

LOBSTER ROLLS

The most expensive hot dog roll you'll ever buy

▶ The common fig would very much like it if you'd all stop calling him common for he believes himself to be extraordinary. Any fig-lover will agree these sweet morsels are a true tease when they appear on greengrocer shelves each year and the clock starts counting down until the season abruptly ends. Not only do figs taste amazing (try them in this salad with crisp lettuce and salty green olives) but they're high in soluble fibre (if you're at an age where that's important) and are packed full of potassium, calcium, magnesium, iron and copper.

▶ Q: How many calories can you cram into a regular size glass?
A: How long is a piece of string?

One of the most recent food trends has been monster shakes or "frankenshakes". The goal appears to be to cram as much ice cream, whipped cream, cookies, marshmallows, brownies, lollies and pretzels on top of an ordinary sized milkshake as you can without the whole thing collapsing.

MONSTER SHAKES

Haters gonna hate but try shakin' these calories off

▶ Most people can relate to this quote, especially in a high-stress cooking situation, like a dinner party, when nothing is going right. Cooking with wine opens up a world of added flavour but there's no need to use the good stuff when adding a drop to a bolognaise sauce, beef stew or chicken casserole. Save the expensive bottles for drinking and stock up on cheaper bottles to saute vegetables in, add to marinades, deglaze a pan with, or just add to a dish to compliment the flavour of the ingredients.

"*I cook with wine. Sometimes I even add it to the food.*"

– W.C. FIELDS

▶ And on the eighth day God said, "let there be nachos!"
Then He looked over the nachos and saw that they were
very good. Then God said, "these nachos could use some
guacamole or something", so He created the avocado.
Praise be unto Him.

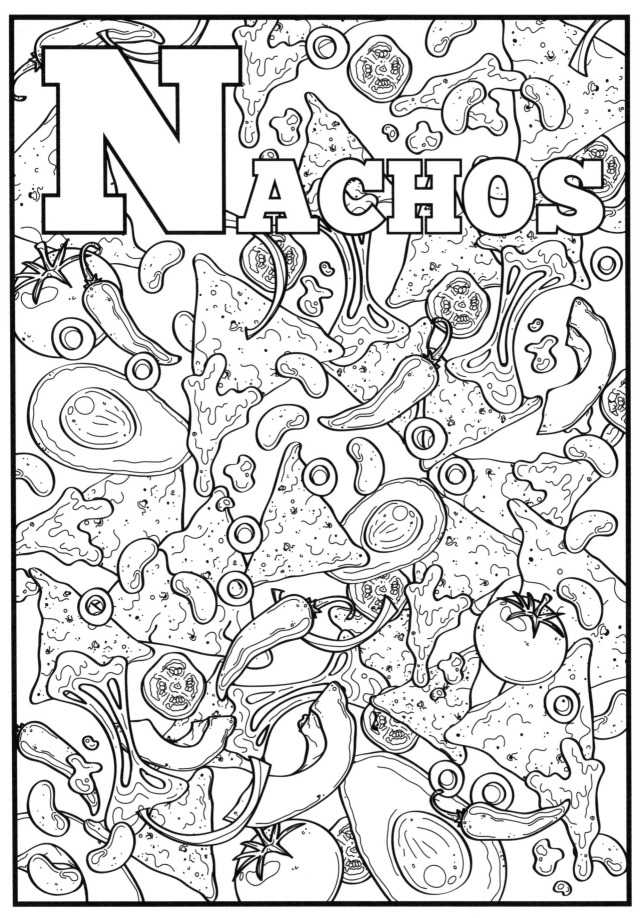

The little black dress of snack foods, always in style

▶ I scream, you scream, we all scream for ice cream! Whether it's ice cream, gelato, frozen yoghurt or sorbet, the tasty treat of frozen milk or cream is a universal one. Origins of the dessert can be traced back to 200BC China. Ice cream became widely popular when entrepreneurs imported ice and established roving street stands, which meant regular foodies didn't need to have their own ice box at home to enjoy the luxurious treat. The latest ice cream food trend is to use liquid nitrogen for a speedy ice cream that's also fun to watch being made.

▶ For years trend predictors have told us that octopus will be a food trend to look out for. So far it hasn't happened on a Cronut level of popularity but that's not too surprising as we all seem to have a sweet tooth for food at the moment. Octopus is abundant and easy to source, it's also a great protein that adopts flavour easily, which makes it prime fodder for experimental chefs to get creative. In the US chefs are pushing the limits with their Octo Dogs - grilled octopus tentacles served in hot dog buns with toppings.

Tasty tentacles touted as the new prawn

▶ Has all this foodie colouring made you peckish? We've selected some favourite sweet treats you can whip up to snack on while you colour. There's a vegan cheesecake, refined sugar free chocolate truffles, and even a beer infused cake that's sure to win you friends if you decide to share it!

SWEET
TREATS

Raspberry ripe "cheesecake"

For those who are after a dairy-free cheesecake this recipe might tempt you. Soaking and blending nuts, such as cashews, to turn into vegan cheeses and butters is nothing new. You'll need a good blender or food processor to whizz the cashews up and ensure a smooth texture akin to cream cheese but the end result is just as satisfying as the traditional recipes.

SERVES 8-10

BASE

1 cup (170g) macadamia nuts
1 cup (80g) shredded unsweetened coconut
¼ cup (60ml) rice malt syrup or maple syrup
¼ cup (60ml) coconut oil, melted

FILLING

2 cups (250g) raw cashews, soaked in water overnight
½ cup (40g) shredded unsweetened coconut
½ cup (125ml) rice malt syrup or maple syrup
1 vanilla bean pod, seeds scraped out
¼ cup (60ml) coconut oil, melted
¼ cup (60ml) coconut milk
¼ tsp sea salt
1 cup (150g) raspberries, fresh or frozen

CHOCOLATE GANACHE

5 tbsp coconut oil
5 tbsp coconut milk
3 tbsp maple syrup
6 tbsp raw cacao powder

TO TOP

1 cup (150g) raspberries, fresh or frozen

To make the base, add the macadamia nuts and coconut to the bowl of a food processor and mix on high until a crumb forms. Add the rice malt syrup and coconut oil and blitz until the mixture is combined and sticks together.

Line a baking tin (any shape) with baking paper and press the mixture into the tin, taking care to push it into the corners and create an even layer. Place the tin in the refrigerator for 30 minutes to set.

To make the filling, rinse the soaked cashews in fresh water, drain, then add to the bowl of a food processor along with the shredded coconut, rice malt syrup, vanilla seeds, coconut oil, coconut milk and sea salt. Mix on high until the filling is silky and smooth, stopping every now and then to scrape down the sides of the bowl. It's important to get the mixture as smooth as possible at this stage as it will guarantee a better texture when it comes to eating the cheesecake later.

Roughly chop the raspberries and gently fold through the filling. Pour the mixture on top of the base and place the tin in the freezer for 2 hours to set.

Prepare the chocolate ganache by melting the coconut oil in a small saucepan and adding the coconut milk and maple syrup. Stir until combined then sift in the raw cacao powder and stir until combined and glossy. Transfer the mixture to a small bowl and refrigerate for 20 minutes until it begins to harden. Transfer the mixture to a piping bag and pipe rounds of the ganache over the top of the cake, alternatively spread the ganache over the top of the cake with a knife.

When ready to serve, scatter the remaining raspberries over the top.

Slice the cheesecake while it's still firm but let the cake sit for 5-10 minutes before serving to allow it to soften slightly.

Choc-berry puff tarts

These are a homemade version of the store bought pop tart variety but slightly healthier. Using premade puff pastry makes these quick to whip up and it's easy to keep the simple ingredients on hand just in case your sweet tooth strikes. Replace the raspberries with other berries or stewed apples or pears for a different flavour.

MAKES 6

2 sheets store bought puff pastry
6 squares of good quality dark chocolate (use flatter/thinner chocolate such as Lindt)
12 fresh raspberries (frozen can be substituted although should be thawed first)
1 egg
Coconut or brown sugar for coating

Preheat the oven to the highest temperature and line an oven tray with baking paper.

Defrost the puff pastry sheets and cut each into three strips (or panels) vertically. Cut the sheet in half horizontally so you end up with six panels.

In the middle of half the pastry panels (these will be base panels) place a square of chocolate and two raspberries.

Whisk the egg and use a pastry brush to dab egg around the edge of each base panel. Place the second pastry panels on top and use a fork to press down around the edges and close the tarts. Brush egg wash over the top of each sealed tart and sprinkle coconut sugar or brown sugar liberally over the top.

Place the tarts on the oven tray and bake for 10 minutes or until puffed up and golden brown. Enjoy warm or cooled.

Mix and match different flavour combinations for the filling.

• Nutella and banana slices
• Peanut butter and fresh strawberries
• Marshmallows and dark chocolate
• Avocado slices and cheddar cheese (omit the coconut sugar on top)

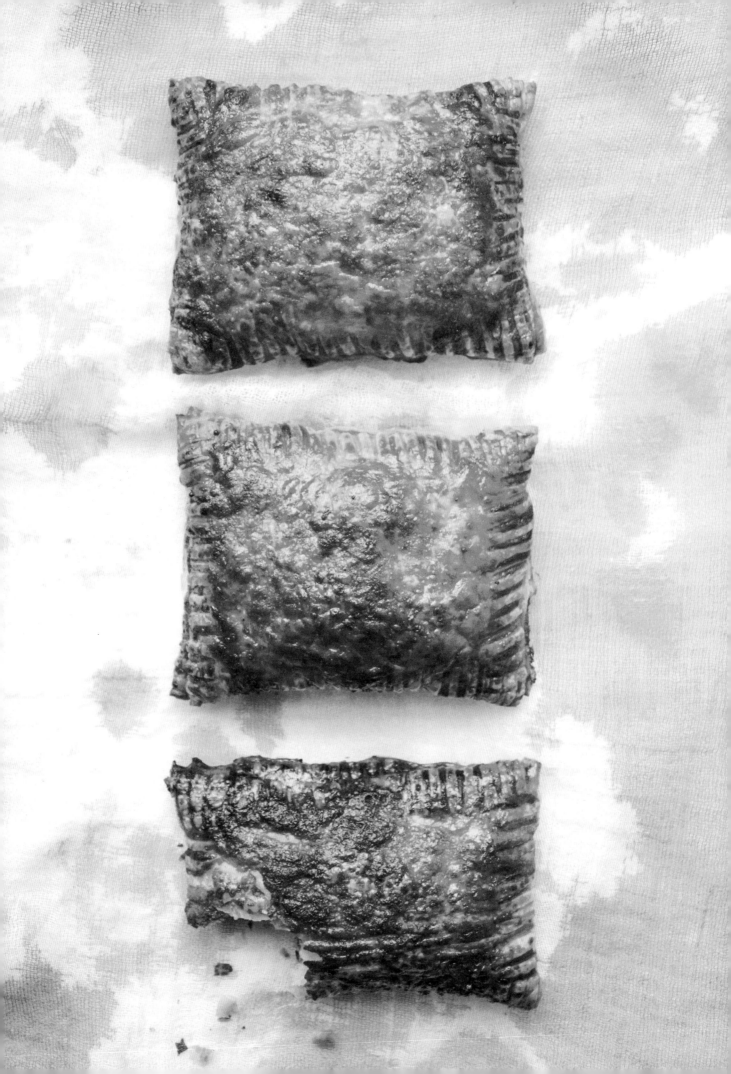

Goji berry + sea salt truffles

Heaven is surely an unlimited supply of raw chocolate truffles while you lounge about on a fluffy cloud. These truffles are not only quick to make but basically fool proof, meaning you throw everything together in a bowl, stick it in the fridge to harden, then roll into bite-size treats that dreams are made of.

MAKES 12

4 tbsp cacao butter
3 tbsp coconut oil
3 tbsp rice malt syrup, honey
  or maple syrup
3/4 cup (90g) raw cacao powder
1 tsp sea salt
1/2 cup (55g) goji berries

COATING
1/3 cup (40g) goji berries
1/4 cup (20g) unsweetened
  shredded coconut

In a small saucepan melt the cacao butter and coconut oil over a low heat. As soon as the mixture turns liquid remove it from the heat and whisk in your sweetener of choice.

Sift in the raw cacao powder and whisk until the mixture is smooth and glossy.

Stir through the sea salt and goji berries then pour the mixture into a shallow bowl and place in the refrigerator for 15-20 minutes.

While the mixture is cooling, prepare the coating to roll the truffles in. Place the goji berries and coconut in the bowl of a food processor and blitz into a powder. Pour the powder over a large plate and set to the side.

When the chocolate mixture has begun to harden, take it out of the fridge and use a teaspoon to scoop up small amounts. Roll the chocolate between your palms into a ball shape, working quickly as your body heat will melt the mixture.

Place the balls on the plate of goji berry powder, roll to coat the outside then place the truffles in an airtight container and store in the refrigerator for up to 2 weeks.

Try:

COFFEE + COCONUT
Mix 1 heaped tbsp of coffee granules into the basic truffle mixture (omitting the sea salt and goji berries from the above recipe) and roll the balls in unsweetened shredded coconut.

BLUEBERRY + GINGER
Mix 1 heaped tbsp of freshly grated ginger and 1/3 cup (50g) of blueberries in the basic truffle mixture and roll the balls in raw cacao powder.

COOKIES + CREAM CRUNCH
Mix 1/2 cup (75g) buckinis with 1 tbsp of raw cacao powder and 1 tbsp of melted coconut oil. Stir the chocolate buckinis through the basic truffle mixture and roll into balls.

For the cream coating, combine 1 cup (250ml) of melted coconut butter with 1 cup (250ml) of melted coconut oil, 1/3 cup (80ml) of rice malt syrup or maple syrup and 1/2 tsp of vanilla powder in a small pan.

Once smooth, gently insert a fork or skewer into each truffle and dip into the mixture, turning to let any excess run off. Place the truffles on a plate lined with baking paper and place in the fridge to set. Store any leftover coconut butter mixture in an airtight container or freeze for next time.

Let's date cake

This moist date and coconut cake can be made in a small tin and sandwiched together with the whipped coconut milk to create a cute mini cake or can be baked in a larger tin to create one large cake and topped with the cream, both are perfect to share.

SERVES 4

250g/9 oz fresh Medjool dates, pitted
1 cup (80g) shredded coconut
½ cup (125ml) melted butter
½ cup (125ml) coconut milk
5 eggs, separated
¾ cup (75g) almond meal
1 tsp ground cinnamon
1 tsp ground ginger
1 tsp vanilla powder

COCONUT FROSTING
1 cup (250ml) coconut milk, refrigerated overnight
Pinch of vanilla powder

Preheat the oven to 170°C/320°F. Grease one large spring form tin or four smaller tins. If you only have one small tin, you can make the cake layers in batches. Place a circle of greaseproof paper on the bottom of the tin to remove the cake easier when cooked.

Blitz the dates and shredded coconut in a food processor before adding the melted butter and coconut milk.

Using a stand mixer or a handheld mixer beat the egg yolks with the cinnamon, ginger and vanilla until just slightly thicker in consistency, approximately 2-4 minutes.

In a large mixing bowl combine the egg yolk mixture with the date mixture then stir the almond meal through gently.

Beat the egg whites in a clean bowl until stiff peaks form. Fold the beaten egg whites gently through the rest of the mixture.

Pour the batter into the prepared tin and bake in the oven for 35-45 minutes or until an inserted skewer comes out clean. Once cooked, let cool for 10 minutes in the tin before turning out onto a wire rack and leaving to cool completely.

Prepare the whipped coconut frosting by whisking (either by hand or using a stand mixer) the coconut milk with a pinch of vanilla powder until thickened. It's best to refrigerate the coconut milk overnight to help it thicken when whisking, however refrigerating for a period of four hours or more will also help. You can replace the coconut milk with unsweetened whipped cream if desired.

Sandwich layers of the cake together with the frosting or pile it atop the cake and garnish with fresh strawberries.

Crispy caramel cups

The peanut butter cup has had its day, it's time for that treat to move over and make way for gooey caramel, crispy quinoa and silky raw chocolate. Date caramel, wholesome quinoa and cacao-rich homemade chocolate are the perfect blend of flavours and textures, you'll be wondering why you didn't combine them before now.

MAKES 12 SMALL

CRISPY QUINOA
1½ tsp extra virgin coconut oil, melted
½ cup (90g) cooked quinoa

DATE CARAMEL
6 Medjool dates, pitted
1 tsp vanilla powder
1 tbsp coconut oil
Pinch of sea salt

RAW CHOCOLATE
½ cup (125ml) extra virgin coconut oil, melted
½ cup (60g) raw cacao powder
1 tbsp maple or rice malt syrup
Pinch of sea salt

Preheat the oven to 180°C/350°F and line an oven tray with baking paper. Mix the melted coconut oil through the cooked quinoa then spread the quinoa out into an even layer on the tray. Bake for 20 minutes, keeping an eye on it and stirring if needed. Once the quinoa is crispy, remove the tray from the oven and set aside to cool.

Prepare the caramel by soaking the dates in boiling water for 10 minutes. Drain then add the pitted dates to the bowl of a food processor with the vanilla powder, coconut oil and sea salt. Blitz until a smooth caramel-coloured mixture comes together.

Prepare the raw chocolate by whisking the coconut oil, cacao powder, rice malt syrup and sea salt together in a bowl until combined.

To make the cups, lay out mini patty pans on a tray or plate. Use a tablespoon or small scoop to pour the base layer of chocolate into each patty pan. Place the tray in the fridge for 5-10 minutes to harden. Remove the tray from the refrigerator and add 1 tsp of the crispy quinoa and 1 tsp of the date caramel to each patty pan. Use the back of the teaspoon to push down on the caramel and create an even layer. Use the remaining chocolate mixture to pour over the top of the caramel. Return the tray to the fridge for 5-10 minutes to set the top layer of chocolate and store in the fridge until ready to eat.

Vanilla cupcakes with chocolate frosting

Looks are one thing but it's what's inside that counts, and this vanilla cupcake with chocolate frosting delivers on taste. These are gluten and refined sugar free but still simple, delicious crowd-pleasers. Decorate the cupcakes with anything of your choosing, from fruits, nuts or seeds to chocolates or lollies.

MAKES 12

½ cup (125ml) coconut butter, melted
1½ cups (375ml) coconut milk
½ cup (125ml) rice malt syrup
1 vanilla bean pod
6 eggs
¾ cup (100g) coconut flour

CHOCOLATE FROSTING
3 tbsp coconut oil
3 tbsp coconut milk
3 tbsp maple syrup or sweetener of choice
3 tbsp raw cacao powder
1 tbsp Dutch cocoa powder
¼ tsp vanilla powder

Fresh fruit, seeds, nuts and coconut to decorate

Preheat the oven to 160°C/320°F.

In a saucepan melt the coconut butter, coconut milk and rice malt syrup together with the beans from the vanilla pod. Take off the heat and set aside.

Separate the egg yolks and whites. Whisk the whites to stiff peaks and set aside. Stir the egg yolks through the cooled coconut mixture followed by the coconut flour.

Lastly, fold the whipped egg whites through the mixture until just combined, taking care not to lose too much air from the mixture.

Use an ice cream scoop to evenly distribute the batter between 12 cupcake liners and bake in the oven for 30 minutes or until an inserted skewer comes out clean. Remove from the oven and cool on a wire rack.

Prepare the frosting by whisking together the coconut oil, coconut milk, rice malt syrup, raw cacao powder, Dutch cocoa powder and vanilla powder until smooth and glossy. Dip each cupcake into the frosting and turn to allow the excess to drip off. Alternatively, place the frosting in the fridge for 5 minutes to firm up then spread over the top of the cupcakes. Top each cupcake with your fruit of choice, such as pomegranate seeds or orange segments, shredded coconut or chopped nuts.

Brooklyn blackberry blackout cake

A traditional blackout cake is a rich, moist chocolate cake with layers of chocolate pudding sandwiching it together. We took this idea and added a stout to the batter to intensify the chocolate flavour. The pudding layers are replaced with fresh whipped cream marbled with plump blackberries that stain the white frosting a striking purple. The tartness of the blackberries pairs beautifully with the rich chocolate cake, making this a real crowd-pleaser treat.

SERVES 10

250g/9 oz butter, cubed
1/2 cup (55g) Dutch cocoa powder
150g/5.3 oz dark chocolate
    (minimum 70% cocoa),
    roughly chopped
1 cup (225g) caster/fine sugar
1 cup (250ml) stout beer
1/2 cup (125ml) buttermilk
2 eggs
1 1/2 cups (225g) plain flour
2 tsp baking soda
2 cups (500ml) cream
2 tbsp icing sugar
1 tsp vanilla powder
300g/10.5 oz blackberries, fresh
    or frozen

Preheat the oven to 170°C/340°F. Line a spring form tin with baking paper on the bottom and sides and set aside.

In a saucepan, add the butter, cocoa, dark chocolate and sugar, stir over a low heat until melted and smooth. Remove the pan from the heat and stir through the beer. Set aside to cool.

In a small bowl whisk together the buttermilk and eggs until combined. Stir through the chocolate mixture until just combined.

Sift the flour and baking soda into the chocolate mixture and fold through gently. Pour the batter into the prepared tin, smooth the top with a spatula and bake in the oven for 45-60 minutes or until an inserted skewer comes out clean. Set aside to cool on a wire rack.

Prepare the frosting by whisking the cream with the icing sugar and vanilla powder until stiff peaks form. Divide the blackberries in half and fold half through the cream gently until evenly distributed.

Serve the cake whole with the whipped cream on top or slice the cake into three even discs and layer together with cream. Save some cream to pile on top and decorate with the remaining blackberries.

Caramel stuffed double nut crunches

These are the perfect balance of savoury and sweet, with the nutty cookies seamlessly complimenting the sticky, sweet date caramel and making it hard to stop at one. What makes these cookies even more tempting is the short list of ingredients, which most people have on hand in the fridge and cupboard.

MAKES 8

1 cup (135g) smooth nut butter
   of choice
1 egg
1/3 cup (80ml) rice malt syrup
   or sweetener of choice
2/3 cup (80g) crushed walnuts
1 tsp ground cinnamon
Sea salt

CARAMEL FILLING
6 Medjool dates, pitted
1 tsp vanilla powder
1 tbsp coconut oil
Pinch of sea salt

Preheat the oven to 180°C/350°F.

In a bowl, stir the nut butter, egg, rice malt syrup, walnuts and cinnamon together. Take spoonfuls of the mixture and roll into balls.

Place on an oven tray lined with baking paper and press down with a fork. Sprinkle the tops of each cookie with a pinch of sea salt. Bake in the oven for 10 minutes.

Prepare the caramel filling by soaking the dates in boiling water for 10 minutes. Drain then add the pitted dates to the bowl of a food processor with the vanilla powder, coconut oil and sea salt. Blitz until a smooth caramel-coloured mixture comes together.

Sandwich two cookies together with a generous spoonful of the caramel filling and store in an airtight container. Any leftover caramel filling can be stored in the fridge for up to two weeks.

Nutty fudge

Sweet treats don't come easier than this recipe that will deliver soft, melt-in-your-mouth fudge in about 30 minutes. Play around with different nuts, dried fruit or seeds, or add flavour with spices such as cinnamon or cayenne pepper.

MAKES 12

1 cup (270g) smooth nut butter
   of choice
1/2 cup (125ml) coconut oil, melted
1 tbsp rice malt syrup
1/2 cup (60g) raw cacao powder
1/2 cup (85g) macadamia nuts

Combine the nut butter, coconut oil, rice malt syrup and raw cacao powder in a bowl, whisk until smooth.

Roughly chop the macadamia nuts and stir through the fudge batter.

Line a shallow brownie tin with baking paper and pour the batter in, smoothing into the corners with a knife. Place in the fridge to set for about 30 minutes before slicing into squares. You can wrap the fudge in squares of greaseproof paper or keep in the tin, store in the fridge until ready to eat.

Metric Conversion Charts

Following a recipe from across the pond? Let these conversion charts help you out!

Converting Ounces to Grams

Ounces	Grams	Ounces	Grams
1 ounce	30 grams	9 ounces	250 grams
2 ounces	60 grams	10 ounces	285 grams
3 ounces	85 grams	11 ounces	300 grams
4 ounces	115 grams	12 ounces	340 grams
5 ounces	140 grams	13 ounces	370 grams
6 ounces	180 grams	14 ounces	400 grams
7 ounces	200 grams	15 ounces	425 grams
8 ounces	225 grams	16 ounces	450 grams

Converting Quarts to Litres

Quarts	Litres
1 cup (¼ quart)	¼ litre
1 pint (½ quart)	½ litre
1 quart	1 litre
2 quarts	2 litres
2 ½ quarts	2 ½ litres
3 quarts	2 ¾ litres
4 quarts	3 ¾ litres
5 quarts	4 ¾ litres
6 quarts	5 ½ litres
7 quarts	6 ½ litres
8 quarts	7 ½ litres

Converting Pounds to Grams and Kilograms

Pounds	Grams; Kilograms
1 pound	450 grams
1 ½ pounds	675 grams
2 pounds	900 grams
2 ½ pounds	1,125 grams; 1 ¼ kilograms
3 pounds	1,350 grams
3 ½ pounds	1,500 grams; 1 1½ kilograms
4 pounds	1,800 grams
4 ½ pounds	2 kilograms
5 pounds	2 ¼ kilograms
5 ½ pounds	2 ½ kilograms
6 pounds	2 ¾ kilograms
6 ½ pounds	3 kilograms
7 pounds	3 ¼ kilograms
7 ½ pounds	3 ½ kilograms
8 pounds	3 ¾ kilograms

Converting Fahrenheit to Celsius

Fahrenheit	Celsius
170	77
180	82
190	88
200	95
225	110
250	120
300	150
325	165
350	180
375	190
400	205
425	220
450	230
475	245
500	260

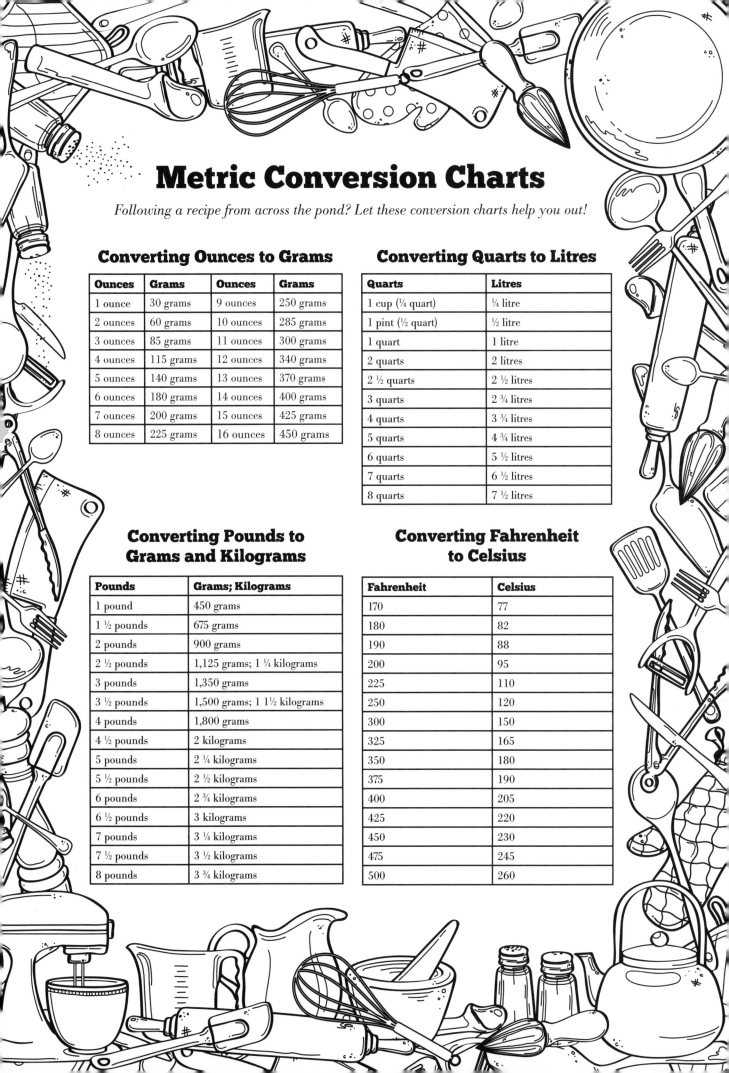

▶ Pickling is not a new food trend, it's an ancient method of preservation that's enjoying a much-deserved revival as thrifty foodies explore the world of fermented and preserved foods. Most people start with something simple like pickled cucumbers or homemade olives but the sky is the limit with a little know-how and a good dose of confidence. For those interested in healthy fermented foods that are great for your gut health, try making your own kimchi or sauerkraut.

What you yell when faced with excess produce

▶ As with any good invention there is dispute over who the true inventor of the salad bar is. For anyone not highly invested in the salad bar industry (i.e. everyone) we'll move on to what makes a salad bar so wonderful. Whether you're faced with an all-you-can-eat scenario or a pay-by-the-weight situation, a fully stocked salad bar is a thing of beauty. Take your pick from a vast array of healthy ingredients such as mushrooms, pickles, olives, cucumber, tomato, boiled egg, capsicum/peppers, artichokes, cheese slices, avocado, and crunchy lettuce.

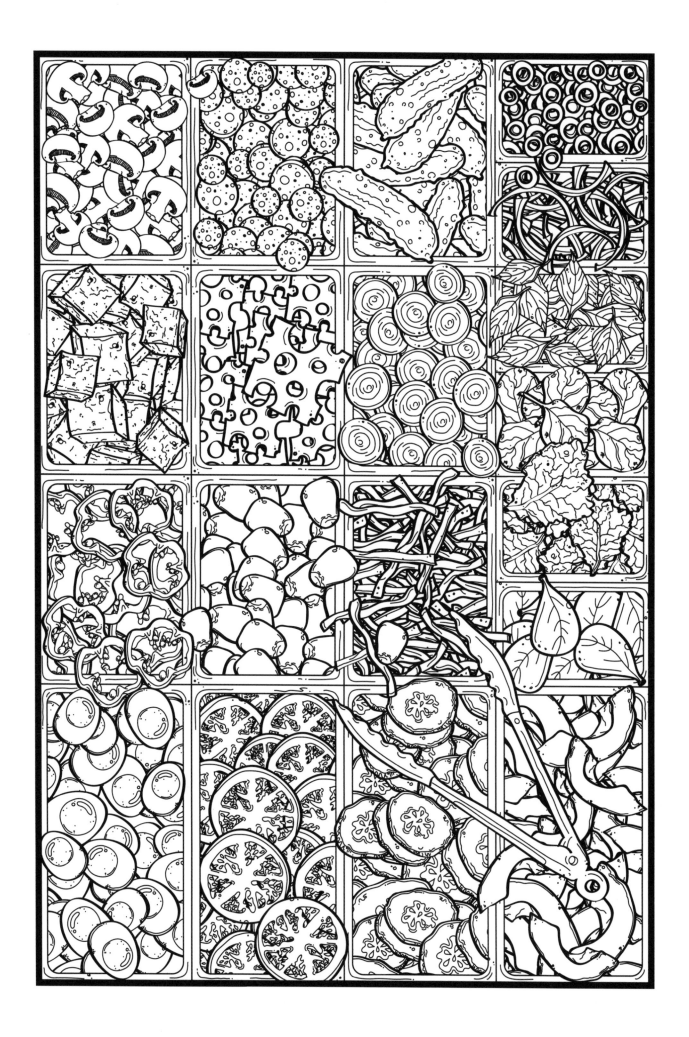

▶ Move over humble chicken egg and make way for the almost too-cute-to-eat quail egg. This speckled delight can be enjoyed fried, scrambled, raw, pickled, smoked or boiled. The taste of quail eggs is not too dissimilar to chicken eggs, although they have a higher yolk to white ratio, but because of their size it takes about 5-6 quail eggs to replace 1 chicken egg in a recipe.

Quail Eggs

Nature's Cadbury Creme Egg

▶ Chicken wings and drumettes are classic beer food, perfect to hold in one hand, a good beer will help cut through the greasiness and enhance the flavours you marinate the chicken in. You can go for the deep fried variety of wings with rich dressings or stick to something a bit lighter with oven baked bites. For an easy marinade, blitz jalapeno peppers, lime juice and coriander/cilantro leaves in the bowl of a food processor with 2 tbsp of rice wine vinegar, ¼ cup (60ml) of extra virgin olive oil and a good pinch of sea salt.

▶ Ramen has long been a favourite food for thrifty
university students but the Japanese noodle soup is fast
expanding and becoming a staple across the world. From
the original bowl to the ramen burger, this cheap, filling
bowl of warming goodness isn't going anywhere fast. A
great ramen restaurant is easily spotted, it's the shop
with a line to get inside.

The noodle soup with a cult following

▶ This tweet by singer-songwriter superstar Dolly Parton to her 3.7 million followers in 2013 garnered just over 3,000 retweets.

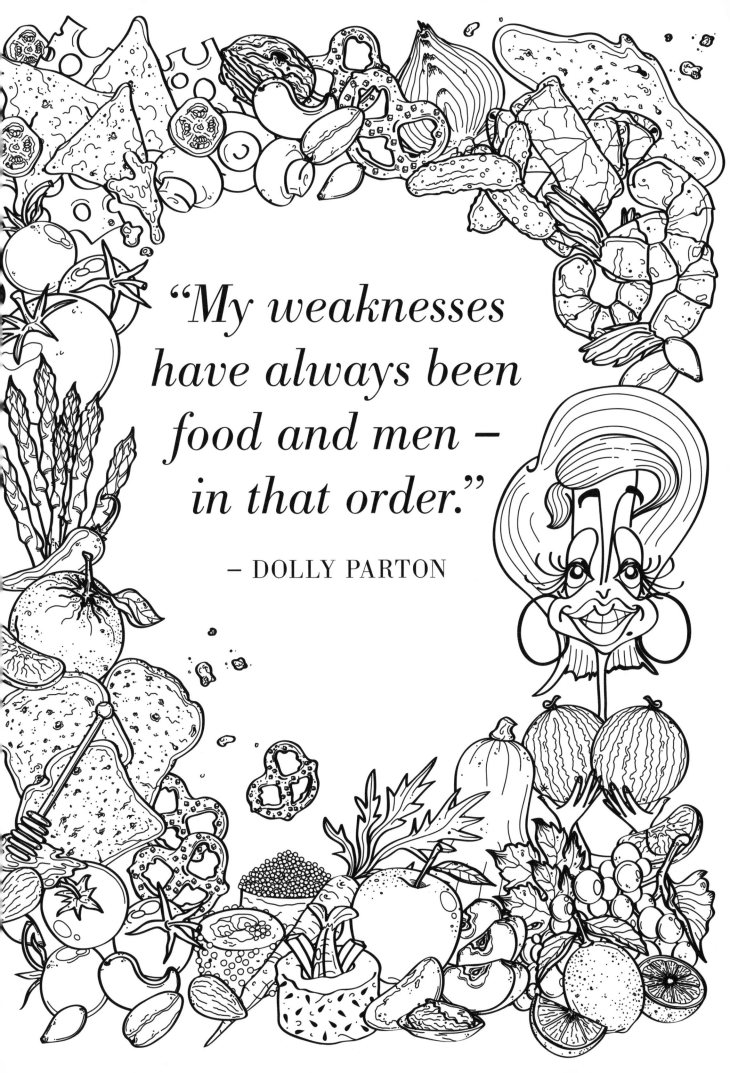

"*My weaknesses have always been food and men – in that order.*"

– DOLLY PARTON

▶ Superfoods may seem like just a buzz word in the foodie world but they still pack a serious nutritional punch, promising high levels of antioxidants and essential nutrients. The term first appeared in the 1990s but gained ground over recent years as our love affair with foods like kale and goji berries exploded. Try adding these superfoods to your diet: broccoli, Brazil nuts, berries, acai, wild salmon and kale.

They're the hero you deserve and the one you need right now

▶ Whether you spell them doughnuts or donuts there's no denying these fried treats are hard to resist. Gourmet doughnuts are definitely on trend in the foodie world, especially with the Cronut craze that swept the world following its creation in New York by pastry chef Dominique Ansel. The croissant-doughnut hybrid saw unprecedented lines outside Ansel's bakery and its limited production led to a black market trade where Cronuts were sold for up to $100 a piece.

▶ Toast is not something most people would think to order when eating out, especially when you have a toaster at home. The new toast trend however may change your mind as cafes and restaurants offer artisanal toast with delicious and interesting flavours. From classics like hazelnut spread with banana to smashed avocado and feta, starting with a good quality bread is a must.

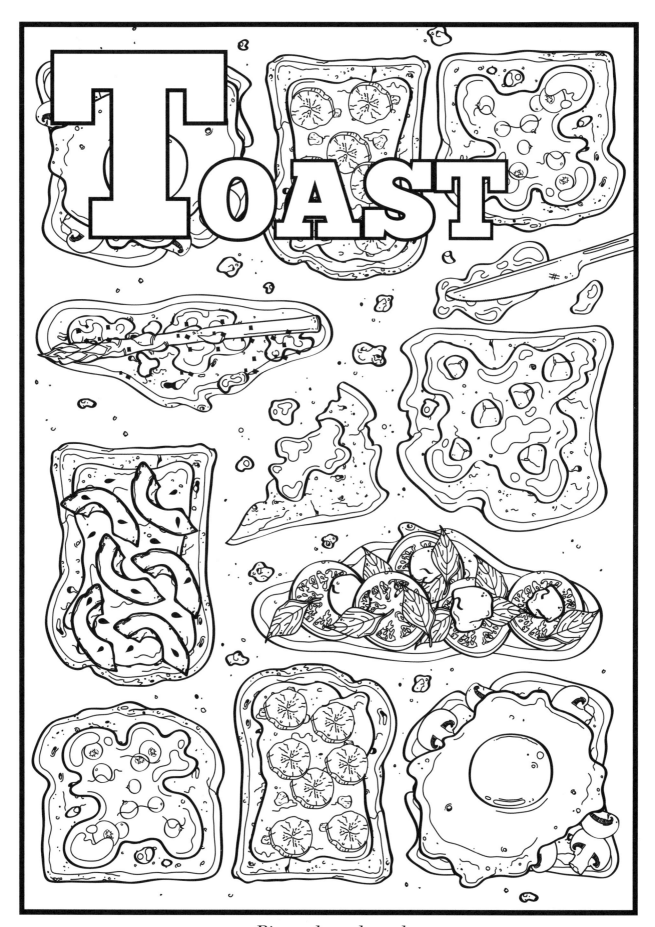

Pimped out bread

▶ The simplest way to impress dinner guests is by placing a loaded antipasto plate in front of them. Faced with a carefully curated selection of cured meats, pickled vegetables, cheese and other bits and pieces, humans have proven themselves incapable of resistance. Antipasto translates to "before the meal" although we think it can be enjoyed as a meal in itself despite what convention says!

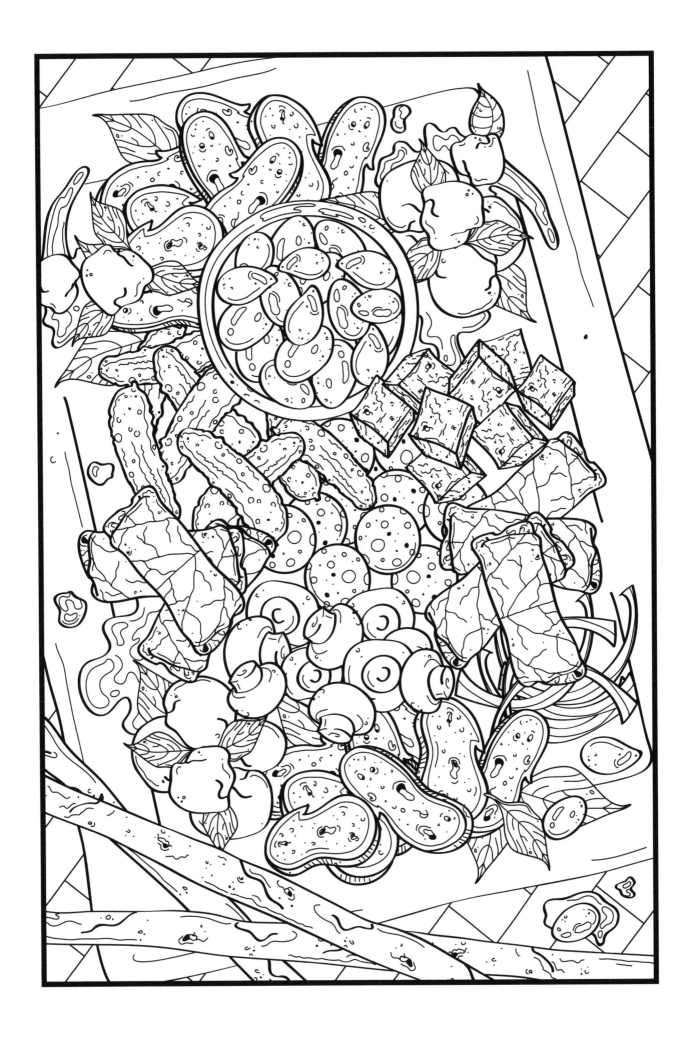

▶ Umami doesn't get the same street cred as sweet, sour, salty or bitter but the fifth basic taste is just as essential. The word umami is Japanese and roughly translates to pleasant savoury taste. Foods rich in umami include cured meats, fish, shellfish, mushrooms, tomatoes, green tea, soy sauce and cheese, such as Parmesan.

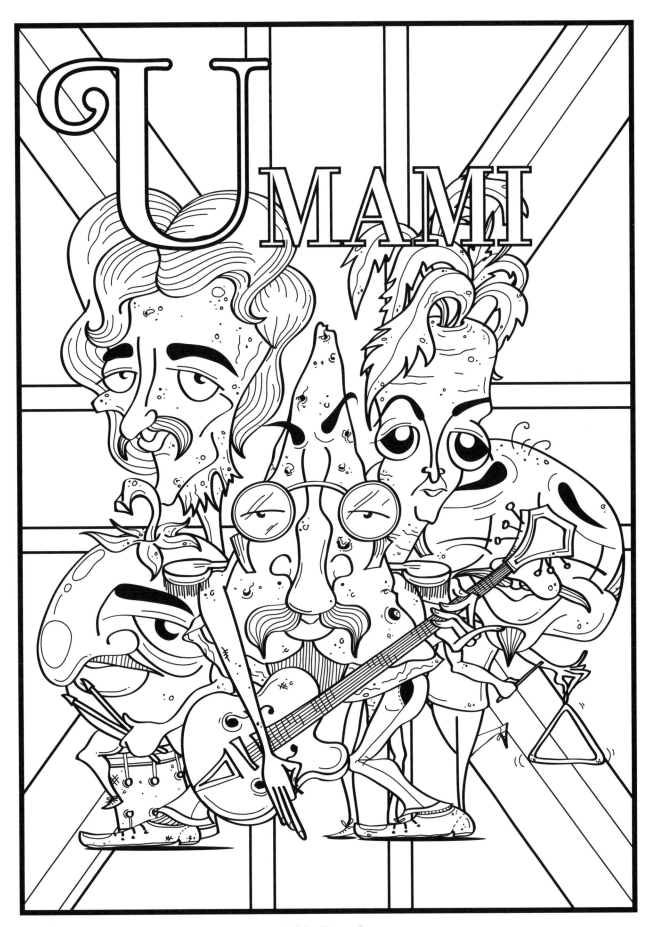

The fifth Beatle taste

▶ Somewhere in the world right now a dentist
is colouring this page in and either weeping at
the destruction candy is wreaking on our teeth
or laughing and putting a downpayment on
a new jet ski.

▶ The ultimate goal for a passionate foodie might be to one day grow their own vegetables, harvest and cook them - true farm to table. While for some people this may seem too out of reach there are urban farming schemes popping up around the world offering a small patch of land for city dwellers to strengthen their green thumb. The easiest produce to grow in small areas and with minimal experience are herbs and leafy greens, once you've mastered those you may want to move on to cucumbers, carrots and tomatoes.

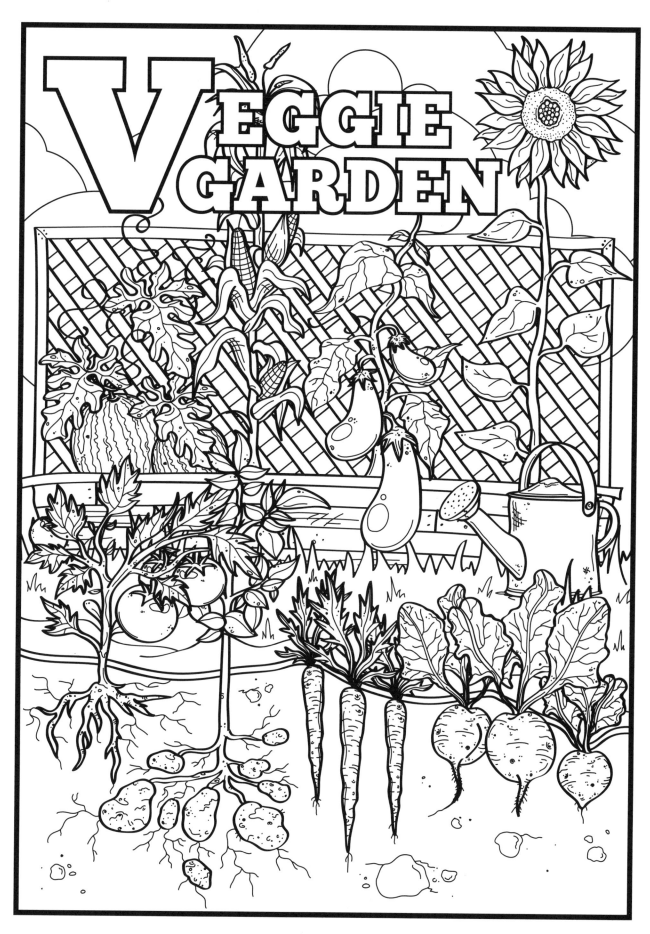

Farm to table just got a lot closer to home

▶ Looking for some pizza topping inspiration? Worldwide the beloved pizza has found a home in our hearts, stomachs and imaginations. If you were in Japan you may find squid and Mayo Jaga (mayonnaise, potato and bacon) atop your crust; visit Brazil and add green peas to your pizza, give a fried egg topping a go in France, try holding down a "mockba" in Russia - a cold pizza topped with mackerel, tuna, sardine, salmon and onion (sounds fab), while the Americans play it a little safer with pepperoni being the number one topping.

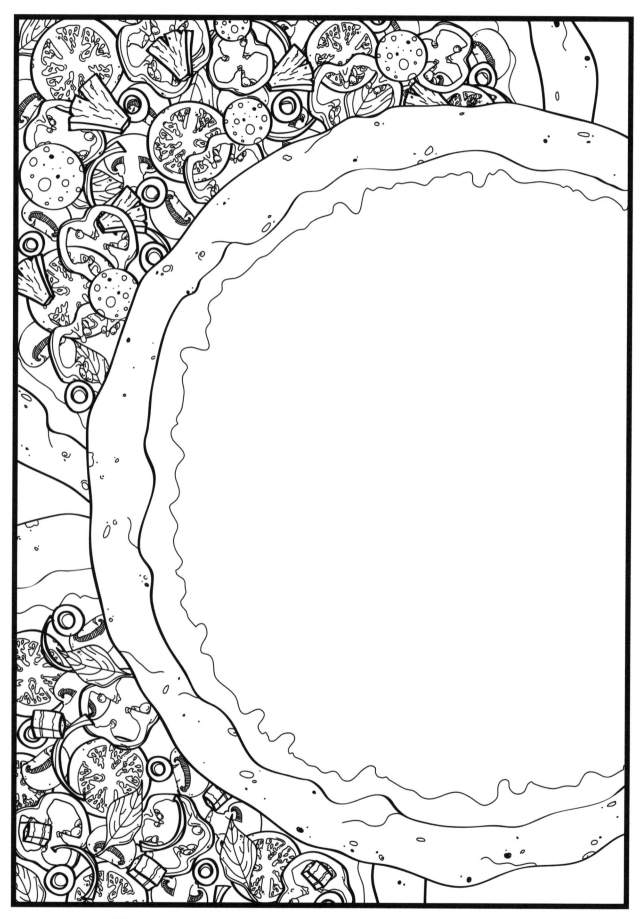

Finish the Drawing: Add the toppings to the pizza

▶ If you want to hear all about lifestyles of the rich and famous look no further than wok stars. They may seem shallow on first impression but they are really quite deep, they'll hold your attention (and your dinner), and they become hotter the more time you spend with them.

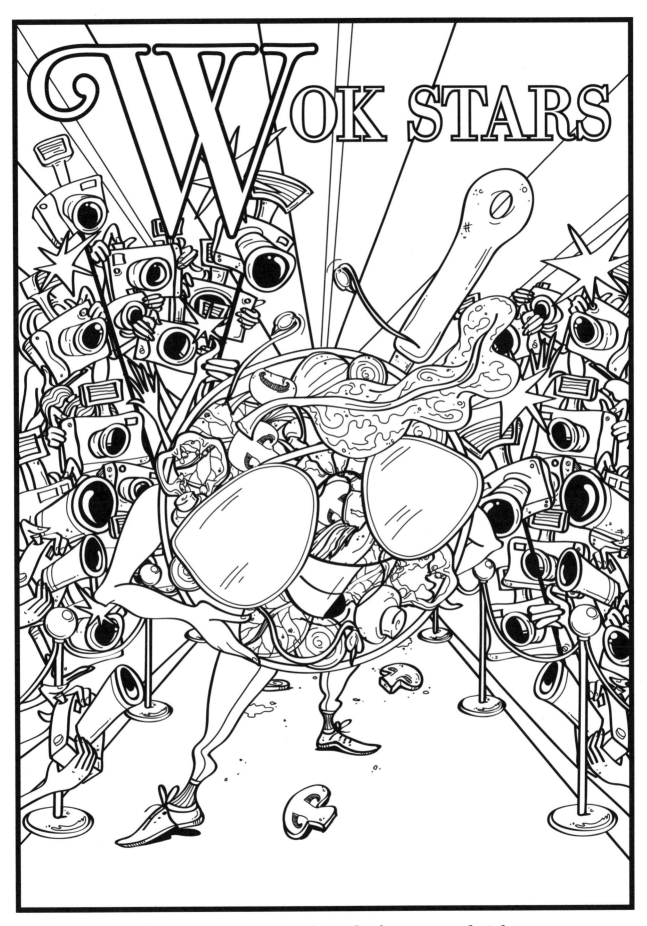

WOK STARS

Just like regular woks only famous and rich

▶ Most of us have grown up with the humble sandwich in our lives. From the soggy tomato sandwich trauma from school days, to gourmet sandwiches, picnic loaves, subs and rolls, it's what's between the two slices of bread that really counts. Stack them low, stack them high, fill them with meat, salad, cheese, sauces and condiments, the sandwich is as versatile as your imagination!

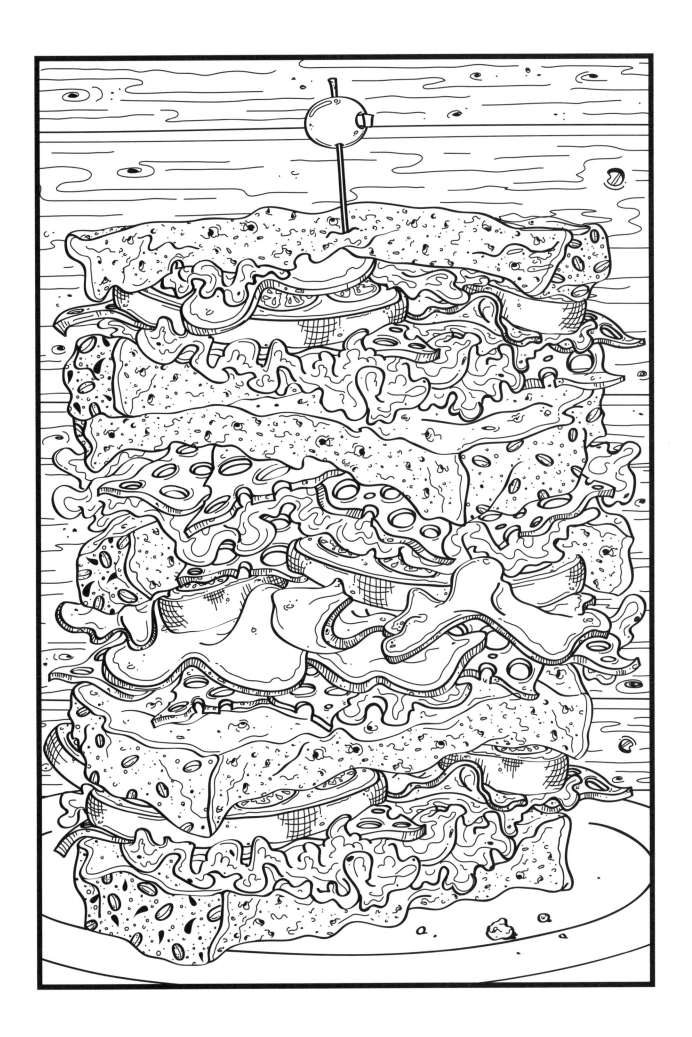

▶ Okay, so we know xanthan gum stars with the letter X but that wouldn't be much fun for you to colour in now would it? Xanthan gum is a food additive and is one of the top 30 additives used in food products. Corn sugar is fermented with a type of bacteria to form a lovely looking goo, it's then dried and ground up into a powder. Xanthan gum is most commonly used as a thickener and emulsifier, and is popular in gluten free products. Pretty happy with that xylophone to colour in now aren't you?

You try thinking of a foodie word that starts with X

▶ While Jonathan Swift is credited with this oyster quote it's only fair to credit the original source that Swift borrowed his words from, Thomas Fuller's Worthies of England. That saying went, "He was a very valiant man who first adventured on eating of oysters". Not quite as punchy as Swift's variation but the sentiment remained in the latter, what must the first oyster-eater have been thinking as he pried open that shell and slurped up the slimy filling?

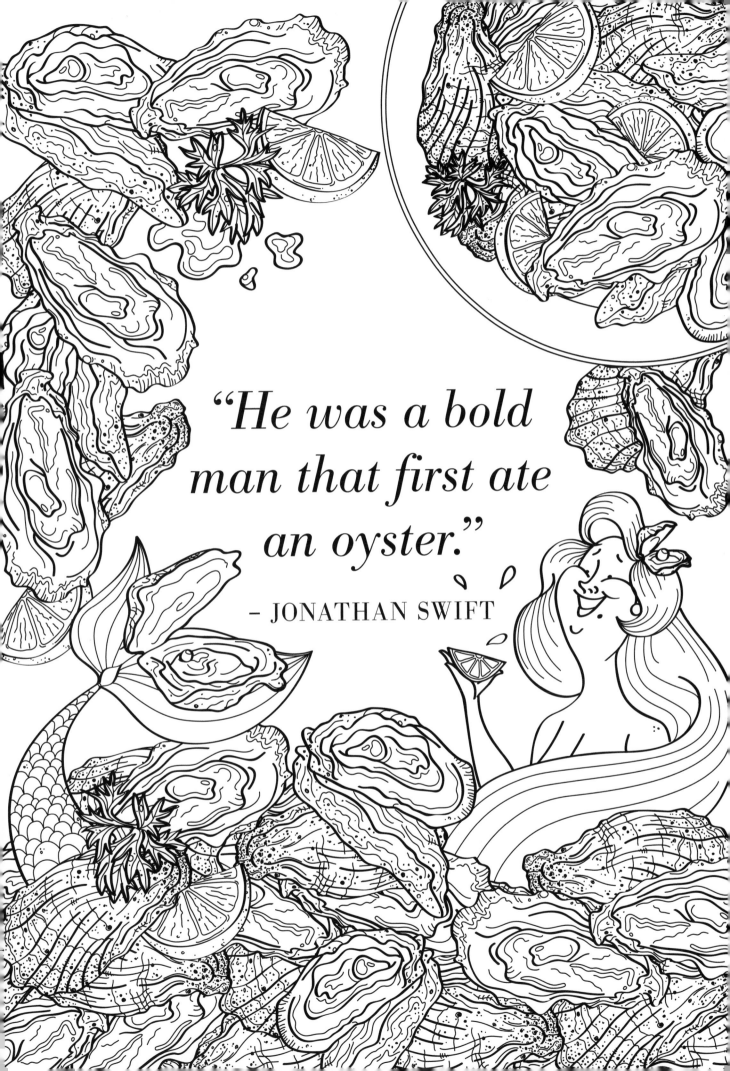

"He was a bold man that first ate an oyster."

– JONATHAN SWIFT

▶ Fruit flavoured yoghurt is a staple in many people's diets but a few ambitious entrepreneurs are banking on foodies being ready to become more adventurous with their yoghurt flavours. Greek yoghurt is a great base to add different flavours to. We add Greek yoghurt to many dishes so why not try mixing some savoury flavours in to the yoghurt itself? Sweeter vegetables such as carrots, pumpkin, sweet potato and beetroot make great additions to plain yoghurt and prep you to push your limits by then trying something like parsnip, dill and tomato, or avocado and spring onion.

Fruit yoghurt is fine but savoury is divine!

▶ Pasta is no longer just a staple of Italian cuisine but of the world. We've all fallen in love with the wheat noodle that comes in myriad of shapes and sizes, and can easily be dressed up in various sauces. There are 310 forms of pasta known by 1300 different names, much more than what's on show at your local supermarket! Foodies may be tempted to try their hand at making fresh pasta at home, they say once you go fresh you never go back!

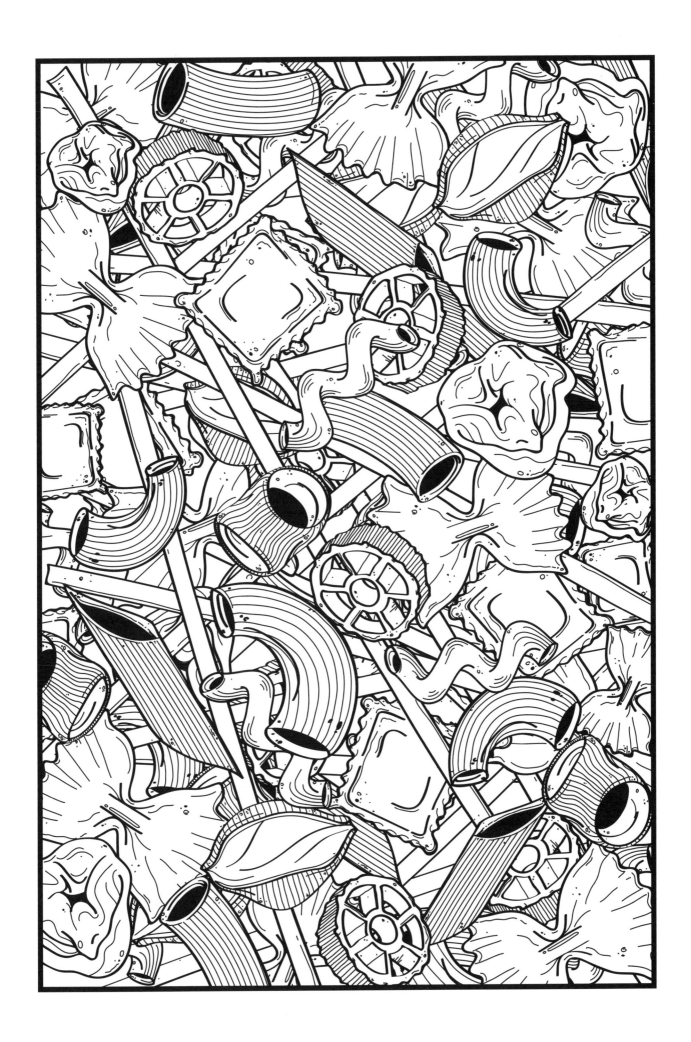

▶ If a dish is missing a certain something then a little citrus zest could be all it needs to lift the flavour. Any serious foodie into home cooking should invest in a quality microplane zester to utlisie the flavour-packed skins on oranges, lemons and limes. Add to salad dressings, curries, stews, salads, over meat or freeze in ice cube trays with water to add flavour to cool drinks.

Oranges and lemons and limes, oh my!

▶ Oven mitts were invented by Earl Mitt in the early 1870s. Really, his surname was Mitt, we're not making this up! It was the permanent disfigurement of his left hand in a baking accident that led him to create the prototype of what we now know as the oven mitt (or glove). The beauty of the oven mitt, apart from protecting your hand against high temperatures, is that you only need to buy one, they fit on either hand!

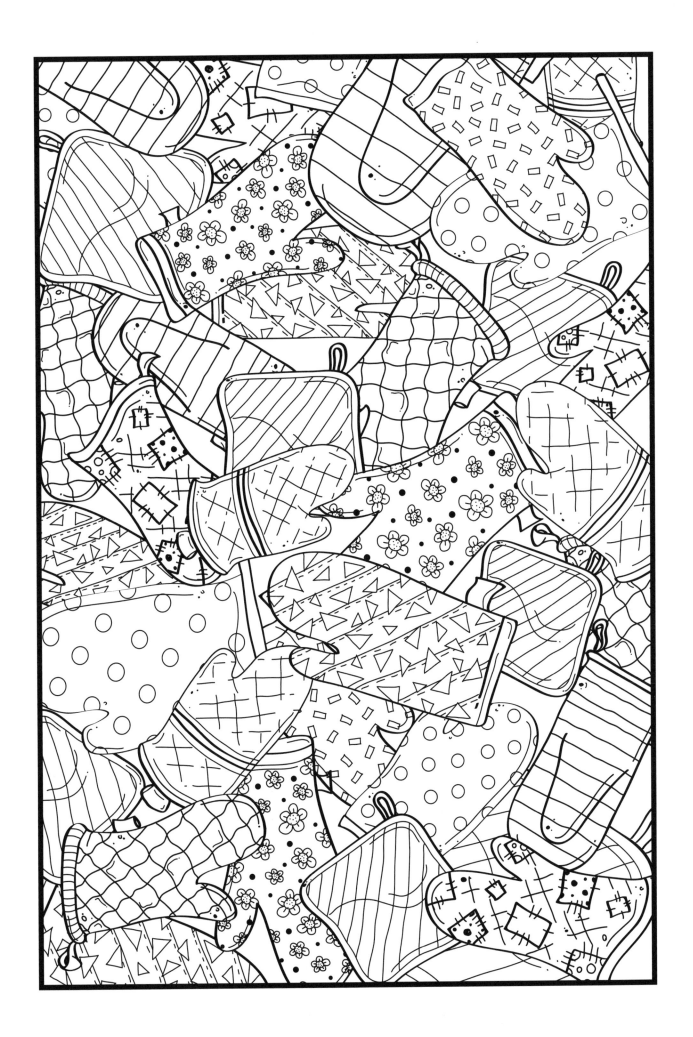

▶ There are some simple ways to jazz up a basic cake with a few special toppings that will surely impress your guests. Take a vanilla or chocolate cake and add chopped pistachios for crunch and flavour. Blitz frozen rapsberries in a food processor until small crumbs form and sprinkle evenly over the top of the cake. Melt good quality chocolate then drizzle over the pistachios and raspberries to finish your masterpiece.

'How much of a foodie are you' results

25-30 Uber foodie

Congratulations you are a supreme foodie who loves everything to do with food. Whether it's eating out at the latest and greatest restaurants, posting your breakfast, lunch, dinner and snacks on Instagram, sampling the hottest new food trend or loading your shopping basket with the finest artisanal products, you are the Queen Bee when it comes to foodies.

15-24 Foodie in training

You love food but you're not an obsessive foodie. You appreciate a great meal and are curious enough to try some of the food trends crossing the globe but you're also happy to keep food as part of your life and not your whole life. You may not be the go-to when it comes to food knowledge but you know enough to keep a dinner party conversation lively.

1-14 Faux foodie

You enjoy food but it's more of a necessity most of the time rather than purely for enjoyment. You don't think your dinner plate deserves to be immortalised online or that a doughnut and croissant should procreate, perhaps you even think that people take their food obsessions a bit too far. You're not a foodie by any stretch of the imagination but you're happy not to be one.